And Then What Happened,
Paul Revere?

DATE	ISSUED TO
APR 23 2001	
JAN 17 2002	
MAR - 6 2002	
MAR 30 2002	
FEB - 6 2003	
OCT 0 4 2005	

DEMCO 32-209

PAUL REVERE , PATRIOT

From the Portrait by John Singleton Copley, ca. 1765

AND THEN WHAT HAPPENED,
PAUL REVERE?

by JEAN FRITZ

PICTURES BY MARGOT TOMES

G. P. Putnam's Sons

The Putnam & Grosset Group

Printed on recycled paper

19 20 18 16 14 12

To Jeremy and Jason

In 1735 there were in Boston 42 streets, 36 lanes, 22 alleys, 1,000 brick houses, 2,000 wooden houses, 12 churches, 4 schools, 418 horses (at the last count), and so many dogs that a law was passed prohibiting people from having dogs that were more than 10 inches high. But it was difficult to keep dogs from growing more than 10 inches, and few people cared to part with their 11- and 12-inch dogs, so they paid little attention to the law. In any case there were too many dogs to count.

Along with the horses, streets, and alleys, there were, of course, people in Boston—more than 13,000. Four of them lived in a small wooden house on North Street near Love Lane. They were Mr. Revere, a gold and silversmith; his wife, Deborah; their daughter, Deborah; and their young son, Paul Revere, born the first day of the new year.

Of all the busy people in Boston, Paul Revere would turn out to be one of the busiest. All his life he found that there was more to do, more to make, more to see, more to hear, more to say, more places to go, more to learn than there were hours in the day.

In Boston there was always plenty to see. Ships were constantly coming and going, unloading everything from turtles to chandeliers. Street vendors were constantly crying their wares—everything from fever pills to hair oil to oysters. From time to time there were traveling acrobats, performing monkeys, parades, firework displays, and fistfights.

Once there was a pickled pirate's head on exhibit; once there was a polar bear.

And there was plenty for Paul to do. When he was fifteen years old, his father died, and Paul took over the silversmithing business. He made beads, rings, lockets, bracelets, buttons, medals, pitchers, teapots, spoons, sugar baskets, cups, ewers, porringers, shoe buckles, and candlesticks.

Once he made a silver collar for a man's pet squirrel.

To make extra money, he took a job ringing the bells in Christ Church. In Boston, church bells were rung not just on Sundays but three times a day on weekdays, at special hours on holidays and anniversaries, for fires and emergencies, whenever a member of the congregation died, and whenever there was especially good news or especially bad news to announce. Sometimes at a moment's notice word would come that the bells were to be rung, and off Paul would run, his hat clapped to his head, his coattails flying.

Busy as he was, Paul liked to do new things. If there was excitement around, he liked to find it. In the spring of 1756, when Paul was twenty-one years old, there was, as it happened, a war close by, and Paul didn't want to miss it. French soldiers, along with Indians, were attacking the borders of the colonies. So Paul grabbed his rifle, buckled on his sword, clapped his hat to his head, and off he went—coattails flying—to defend Fort William Henry on Lake George.

And what happened?

Paul spent the summer sitting around, cleaning his rifle and polishing his sword. And swatting flies. There were thousands of flies at Lake George that summer. But there were no French or Indians.

In November the Massachusetts men were sent home. Paul went back to Boston, married Sarah Orne, and began filling up his house with children. There were

Deborah, Paul, Sarah, Mary, Frances, and Elizabeth (in addition to two babies who died young). Then Sarah

died, and Paul married Rachel Walker, and along came Joshua, Joseph, Harriet, Maria, and John (in addition to three more babies who died young).

Paul kept putting up new chairs at the kitchen table, and now in addition to making buckles, spoons, cups, and all the other silver items, Paul had to find new ways to make money. So he engraved portraits, produced bookplates, sold pictures, made picture frames, brought out hymnbooks, and became a dentist. "Artificial Teeth. Paul Revere," he advertised. "He fixes them in such a Manner that they are not only an Ornament, but of real Use in Speaking and Eating."

You would think that with all Paul Revere did, he would make mistakes. But he always remembered to put spouts on his teapots and handles on his cups.

The false teeth that he whittled out of hippopotamus tusk looked just fine.

Generally when he did arithmetic in his Day Book, he got the right answers.

Of course, sometimes there were so many different things to do that he forgot what he was doing. In the beginning of a new Day Book, he wrote, "This is my book for me to—", but he never finished the sentence.

Sometimes he was in such a hurry that his writing looked sloppy. At the end of a letter he would write, "Pray excuse my scrawl."

Sometimes he was late for his work. There was a hymnbook, for instance, that didn't come out until eighteen months after he had promised it.

Once he built a barn and by mistake put part of it on a neighbor's property.

Still, Paul Revere wasn't always at work. Occasionally he just dreamed. There was one page in his Day Book that he used simply for doodling.

But beginning in 1765, there was no time for doodling. The French had stopped bothering America, but now the English were causing trouble, telling the colonies they couldn't do this and couldn't do that, slapping on taxes, one after another. First there was a tax on printed matter—newspapers, diplomas, marriage licenses. When this was withdrawn, there was a tax on tea, glass, printers' colors, and paper. The one tax England would never give up was the tax on tea.

And what did Paul Revere do about it?

He became a leader of the Sons of Liberty, a secret club that found interesting ways to oppose the English.

One of Paul's busiest nights was December 16, 1773. He prepared for it by smearing his face with red paint and lampblack, pulling a tight stockinglike covering over his head, and draping a ragged blanket over his shoulders. Then he picked up his ax and joined other Sons of Liberty, all pretending to be Indians, all carrying axes.

And what were they up to?

They were going to make sure that no one in Boston would pay taxes on the three shiploads of tea that had just arrived from England. So they marched on board the ships, hauled the chests of tea onto the decks, broke them open with their axes, and dumped the tea—10,000 pounds of it—into Boston Harbor. It was all done in an orderly fashion. No one was hurt; no other cargo was touched; the ships were unharmed. (There was only one minor incident when a man, found stuffing tea into the lining of his coat, had to be punished.)

When the Sons of Liberty finished, they marched home, washed their faces, and went to bed.

But not Paul Revere. Someone had to ride to New York and Philadelphia and spread the news. And Paul was picked to do it.

So off he galloped, his hat clapped to his head, his coattails flying. From Boston to Cambridge to Watertown to Worcester to Hartford *(watch out, dogs on the road! watch out, chickens!)* to New York to Philadelphia he went. And back. 63 miles a day. (This was not swatting flies!)

He was back in Boston on the eleventh day, long before anyone expected him.

Paul Revere became Massachusetts' Number One express rider between Boston and Philadelphia. He also became a secret agent. In the winter of 1774 it looked more and more as if the English soldiers in Boston meant to make war on America, and Paul's job was to try to find out the English plans.

He was far too busy now to write in his Day Book. He was too busy to make many silver teapots or to whittle many teeth. Instead, he patrolled the streets at night, delivered messages to Philadelphia, and kept himself ready at all times to warn the countryside.

Sometimes on his missions things went just right. He got past the sentries, got through the snow, kept his horse on the road, and kept himself on his horse.

Sometimes things went poorly. Once the English found him in a rowboat snooping around Castle Island in Boston Harbor. So they stopped him, questioned him, and locked him up. He stayed locked up for two days and three nights.

But all his rides, Paul knew, were small compared to the Big Ride that lay ahead. Nothing should go wrong with this one. In the spring, everyone agreed, the English would march into the countryside and really start fighting. And when they did, Paul Revere would have to be ahead of them.

On Saturday, April 15, spring, it seemed, had arrived. Boats for moving troops had been seen on the Charles River. English scouts had been observed on the road to Lexington and Concord. A stableboy had overheard two officers making plans.

At 10:45 on Tuesday night, April 18, Dr. Joseph Warren, who was directing Patriot activities in Boston, sent for Paul Revere. Other messengers had been dispatched for Lexington and Concord by longer routes. Paul was to go, as planned, the same way the English were going

—across the Charles River. He was to alarm the citizens so they could arm themselves, and he was to inform John Hancock and Samuel Adams, Boston's two Patriot leaders who were staying in Lexington. And Paul was to leave now.

He had already arranged a quick way of warning the people of Charlestown across the river. Two lanterns

were to be hung in the steeple of the North Church if the English were coming by water; one lantern if they were coming by land.

So Paul rushed to the North Church and gave directions. Two lanterns, he said. Now.

Then he ran home, flung open the door, pulled on his boots, grabbed his coat, kissed his wife, told the children to be good, and off he went—his hat clapped to his head, his coattails flying. He was in such a hurry that he left the door open, and his dog got out.

On the way to the river Paul picked up two friends, who had promised to row him to the other side. Then all three ran to a dock near the Charlestown ferry where Paul had kept a boat hidden during the winter. Paul's dog ran with them.

The night was pleasant, and the moon was bright. Too bright. In the path of moonlight across the river lay an armed English transport. Paul and his friends would have to row past it.

Then Paul realized his first mistake. He had meant to bring cloth to wrap around the oars so the sound would be muffled. He had left the cloth at home.

That wasn't all he had left behind. Paul Revere had started out for his Big Ride without his spurs.

What could be done?

Luckily, one of Paul's friends knew a lady who lived nearby. He ran to her house, called at her window, and asked for some cloth. This lady was not a time waster. She stepped out of the flannel petticoat she was wearing and threw it out the window.

Then for the spurs. Luckily, Paul's dog was there, and luckily, he was well trained. Paul wrote a note to his wife, tied it around the dog's neck, and told the dog to go home. By the time Paul and his friends had ripped the petticoat in two, wrapped each half around an oar, and launched the boat the dog was back with Paul's spurs around his neck.

Paul and his two friends rowed softly across the Charles River, they slipped carefully past the English transport with its 64 guns, and they landed in the shadows on the other side. Safely. There a group of men from Charlestown who had seen the signal in the church steeple had a horse waiting for Paul.

And off Paul Revere rode on his Big Ride.

He kept his horse on the road and himself on his horse, and all went well until suddenly he saw two men on horseback under a tree. They were English officers. One officer sprang out and tried to get ahead of Paul. The other tried to overtake him from behind, but Paul turned his horse quickly and galloped across country, past a muddy pond, toward another road to Lexington.

And what happened to the officers?

One of them galloped straight into the mud and got stuck; the other gave up the chase.

Paul continued to Lexington, beating on doors as he went, arousing the citizens. At Lexington he woke up John Hancock and Samuel Adams and advised them to leave town. He had a quick bite to eat, and then, in the company of two other riders, he continued to Concord, warning farmers along the way.

For a while all went well. And then suddenly from out of the shadows appeared six English officers. They rode up with their pistols in their hands and ordered Paul to stop. But Paul didn't stop immediately.

"Damn you, stop!" one of the officers shouted. "If you go an inch farther, you are a dead man."

Paul and his companions tried to ride through the group, but they were surrounded and ordered into a pasture at one side of the road. What was more, they were told to move quickly if they didn't want their brains blown out.

In the pasture six other officers appeared with pistols in their hands.

One of them spoke like a gentleman. He took Paul's horse by the reins and asked Paul where he came from.

Paul told him, "Boston."

The officer asked what time he had left Boston.

Paul told him.

The officer said, "Sir, may I crave your name?"
Paul answered that his name was Revere.
"What! *Paul* Revere?"
Paul said, "Yes."
Now the English officers certainly did not want to let Paul Revere loose, so they put him, along with other prisoners, at the center of their group, and they rode off toward Lexington. As they approached town, they heard a volley of gunfire.
"What was that?" the officer asked.
Paul said it was a signal to alarm the countryside.
With this piece of news, the English decided they'd like to get back to their own troops in a hurry. Indeed, they were in such a hurry that they no longer wanted to be bothered with prisoners. So after relieving the prisoners of their horses, they set them free.

And then what happened?

Paul Revere felt bad, of course, to be on his Big Ride without a horse. He felt uneasy to be on a moonlit road on foot. So he struck out through the country, across stone walls, through pastures, over graveyards, back into Lexington to see if John Hancock and Samuel Adams were still there.

They were. They were just preparing to leave town in John Hancock's carriage. Paul and Hancock's clerk, John Lowell, went with them.

All went well. They rode about two miles into the countryside, and then suddenly John Hancock remembered that he had left a trunk full of important papers in a Lexington tavern. This was a mistake. He didn't want the English to find those papers.

So what happened?

Paul Revere and John Lowell got out of the carriage and walked back to Lexington.

It was morning now. From all over the area farmers were gathering on Lexington Green. As Paul crossed the green to the tavern, there were between 50 and 60 armed men preparing to take a stand against the English. The troops were said to be near.

Paul went into the tavern, had a bite to eat, found the trunk, and carried it out, holding one end while

John Lowell held the other. As they stepped on the green, the troops appeared.

And then what happened?

Paul and John held onto the trunk. They walked right through the American lines, holding onto the trunk. They were still holding on when a gun was fired. Then there were two guns, then a succession of guns firing back and forth. Paul did not pay any attention to who was firing or who fired first. He did not stop to think that this might be the first battle of a war. His job was to move a trunk to safety, and that's what he did.

The battles of Lexington and Concord did, of course, begin the Revolutionary War. And they were victories for the Americans who have talked ever since about Paul Revere's ride. Some things went well on Paul's ride, some things went poorly, but people have always agreed that the ride was a success.

But now that the war had started, what did Paul Revere do?

Naturally, he kept busy. He rode express for the Committee of Safety, for which he was paid 4 shillings a day. (He had asked for 5.) He printed paper money for the colony, engraved its official seal, supervised the setting up of a powder mill, learned how to make brass and iron cannon, and took part in two military engagements—one in Rhode Island, one in Maine. And as a lieutenant colonel in the Massachusetts militia, he was put in command of the fort at Castle Island.

Some things went well for Paul during the war. Some things went poorly—the same as always.

At the end of the war Paul was 48 years old. He went back to silversmithing, but this wasn't enough to keep him occupied. So he opened a hardware store. In addition to hardware, he sold sandpaper, playing cards, woolen cloth, sealing wax, fish lines, wallpaper, pumice stones, pencils, and spectacles. (Once he sold Samuel Adams two dozen sleigh bells.)

Later he set up a foundry and made stoves, anvils, forge hammers, bolts, cogs, braces and pumps.

Then he began to make church bells. He made 398 bells, most of them weighing at least 500 pounds. He charged 42 cents a pound for them and often had trouble collecting his bills. (75 of his bells still ring in New England steeples.)

Still later he learned how to roll sheet copper, set up a rolling mill, and made copper sheathing for ships. And when the dome of Boston's new Statehouse was built, Paul gave it a shiny copper covering.

But Paul Revere was not always at work. Sometimes he just dreamed. Sometimes he would go back in his mind to the days when he was Massachusetts' Number One express rider. Then, if anyone were around, Paul would talk about his Big Ride. He even wrote out the story of his ride—in a hurry, of course, for the writing looked sloppy.

Boston was not the same as it had been when Paul was a young man. No one bothered now to count the streets and the alleys, the horses and houses. They were too busy putting up new buildings, tearing down hills, filling in ponds, building bridges, and making the city bigger. They still did count the people, however. In 1810, when Paul was 75 years old, there were 33,787

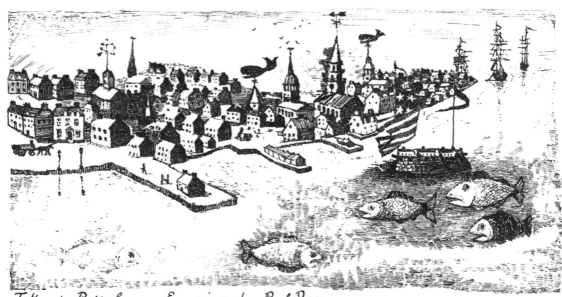

Taken, in Part, from an Engraving by Paul Revere

people in Boston. Nineteen of these were Paul's grandchildren. He also had great-grandchildren, but no one bothered to keep a record of them. But it was the great-grandchildren, more than anyone else, who liked being around when Paul told his story. If he paused or if he appeared to be reaching an end, they would urge him to keep on.

"And then what happened?" they would ask.

"And *then* what happened?"

Notes from the Author

Sometimes readers like to know more than can actually be fitted into a story. Here are additional facts about what happened on some of the pages of this book.

Page

22 Everything went just right the night that Paul Revere rode to Portsmouth, New Hampshire, to warn the citizens that the English were sending troops to reinforce the fort there. Before the English arrived, the citizens of Portsmouth captured the fort, tied up the commander, and hauled down the English flag.

25 Paul was snooping around Castle Island because he had heard that English soldiers were going to Salem in the hope of capturing an American cannon. They made their expedition while Paul was locked up, but fortunately they didn't find the cannon.

Dr. Warren sent William Dawes to Lexington and Concord by the roundabout land route. William was a good actor and frequently got past sentries by pretending he was either a drunken or retarded farmhand.

28 In his written account of his ride, Paul did not mention that he forgot the cloth and his spurs. This was added to the story later by a granddaughter, who said that was the way Paul Revere had told her the story.

34 William Dawes was one of the riders who joined Paul at Lexington. Before the English let the prisoners go, William, in an attempt to get free, fell off his horse. In the process he lost his watch. Several days later he returned to the spot and found the watch just where he'd dropped it.

All the conversation of the English officers is just as Paul Revere himself recorded it.

41 The Americans lost a total of 93 men at Lexington and later at Concord. The English lost 273.

In addition to the trunk, Samuel Adams and John Hancock left behind a fresh salmon which they had just been given—one of the first of the year, a treat they had been looking forward to. It wasn't worth going back for, of course, but even while they were escaping the English soldiers, John and Samuel talked about that salmon.

John Hancock's trunk is now in the Museum of the Worcester Historical Society in Worcester, Massachusetts.

42 Paul had always wanted to be an officer in the Continental Army and felt bitter that his appointment was only in the Massachusetts militia. Indeed, his military life was a disappointment in many ways. Both the expeditions to Rhode Island and Maine were failures. Moreover, in the general confusion and retreat in the Maine affair, Paul was accused of disobedience and cowardice. The Navy officers who accused him were obviously trying to put the blame on the land officers, but in any case Paul was relieved of his command. Paul insisted on a formal court-martial, and his name was finally cleared.

45 Paul Revere died in 1818 at the age of 83.

About the Author

JEAN FRITZ was born in Hankow, China, where her father was a missionary. As a child, she decided to be a writer and write stories about Americans. She has lived up to her determination.

Her well-known works of historical fiction include *The Cabin Faced West, Brady, I, Adam, Early Thunder,* and *George Washington's Breakfast.*

Jean Fritz is also the author of several picture books for younger readers, of which *Fish Head* was the first, and an adult novel, *Cast for a Revolution.* She often reviews children's books for the New York *Times.*

Mrs. Fritz has two children and lives in Dobbs Ferry, New York.

About the Artist

With her illustrations for *Aaron and the Green Mountain Boys* and *The Secret of the Sachem's Tree,* both Junior Literary Guild selections, Margot Tomes has become increasingly noted for her superb illustrations of the Colonial period.

A graduate of Pratt Institute, Miss Tomes was born in Yonkers, New York. She has also illustrated such books as *Joe and the Talking Christmas Tree, Plenty for Three,* and *A Secret House.* In addition to being a children's book illustrator, she is a textile designer.

Miss Tomes lives and works in New York City.